STAY
COOLER
4 Less Money

BUFF BROWN
Foremost Expert on Evaporative Coolers

STAY
COOLER
4 Less Money

BUFF BROWN
Foremost Expert on Evaporative Coolers

First Edition: October 12th, 2014. Proudly printed in the USA.
Published by: Abundant Press
Co-Editors: Pamela Brown, Chris Brown, Stan Barnes, and Karyn Barnes
Back cover photo by: Andy Broadaway
ISBN #: 978-0692349847

Trademarks
All terms mentioned in this book that are known to be trademarks or service marks have been appropriately capitalized. Trademarks belong to the appropriate companies.

Thank you for investing in

Your education by purchasing this book.

Register this book

& receive additional bonuses at:

www.EvaporativeCoolerBook.com

Table of Contents

Acknowledgements

This book was written in two months. However, it was the first 30 years of hard work and over 25,000 customers, clients and friends that made it all possible. Thank you!

First to my incredible wife, Pamela, who for the last 35 years of my life has always stood by me no matter what challenges we faced. Pam, you're an amazing woman and I thank God every day for you. To my two incredible boys Shawn & Christopher, who are not only two great men, but also my best friends. I thank you all for the amazing life you have given me. I love you all very much.

Tony and Sage Robbins: Bula, Bula! Thank you for your passion, wisdom and inspiration. You have given my family and millions of others the reason to live life with passion every day, and to see things as they are, not worse than they are, and to look at every problem as a gift, not a curse, and to make something extraordinary from it.

Mike Koenigs for your passion to help all of us to be better marketer's in delivering our message. Without you this book would not have happened. You showed me how I can have Me, Now, Everywhere in the market place.

To Andy Broadaway for your passion and foresight which made this book possible by taking massive action and being committed to my success. Most of all, thank you for your friendship.

To Jimmy Harding who introduced me to this awesome family called Instant Customer. Thank you for your patience, wisdom and guidance, showing me how to take my business to the next level.

Thank you to my amazing team members past and present that helped Desert Cooler Specialist become the utmost expert in evaporative cooling. Thank you Scott McNeil, Curtis Carver, and Joe Dominguez for your passion for helping our customers stay comfortable without going broke.

To all my customers and clients over the past 30 years that have let us become a part of your life and trusting us with your comfort. Most of all, thank you for your friendship. Without you we would be nothing more than just another service company. Thank You!

And to everyone else that I may have forgotten to give thanks and praise to, thanks for the amazing life and business opportunity you allowed me to have. We could not have stuck around for 30 years without you.

Who Is Buff?

I'm Buff Brown. I live in
Palm Springs, California,
and have done so for close
to 50 years. I moved here
in 1962 from Salt Lake
City, Utah. I was
introduced to using
swamp coolers as a means
of cooling our home in the
early 60's. As a young man in high school wanting to
work, I was taken on by my best friend's father, Mickey
Albright, who had a small swamp cooler company
which bore his name; Mickey Albright's Desert Coolers
– this is back in the early '70's.

Mickey serviced and installed swamp coolers. We drove
around in a blue 1956 Ford pickup truck that had
wooden boxes mounted on both sides, a ladder sticking
out the back, and no air-conditioning. It was very
primitive but we got the job done.

I worked for Mickey during the summer months as a part-time job to get some extra cash. Not knowing at the time he was teaching me values and a trade that would serve me throughout my life. Mickey was strict and always told me, "Look, if you're going to do a job, do it right the first time or don't do it at all." That philosophy has stuck with me to this day, not only in my business, but in my personal life as well.

I worked for Mickey for a couple of summers and after completing two years of college, I decided to move to Newport Beach, California to work in a restaurant called Bobby McGee's. Everything was going great in Newport Beach. I had a great job, was making great money and was having a blast. However, one day I got a phone call from my best friend Mike, Mickey's son who said, "My father just passed away. I need you to come back and help me run his company; I'm going to take it to another level." I said, "Great, let's grow this company."

I came back to Palm Springs and we started growing the company. As we grew the business Mike realized that it was time to get his contractor's license to add air conditioning and heating into the business. When Mickey had his company, he wasn't a licensed contractor and the air-conditioning companies loved him for it; they hated working on swamp coolers and would refer all of their business to him. The Contractor's Board was always pressuring Mickey to get his contractor's license. However, the air-conditioning companies convinced the Contractor's Board he didn't need a license by saying, "Hey look guys, leave him alone, he's just working on swamp coolers. We hate working on swamp coolers and he's doing us a huge favor, so just leave him alone." And they did.

As the company grew we realized we needed to know how to bend and fabricate sheet metal. Mike bought some sheet metal equipment and we both taught ourselves how to layout and "break" (bend) sheet metal. Learning how to manipulate sheet-metal was quite comical because every time we went into the shop we came out covered in Band-Aids due to the fact we had cut ourselves so much. We learned very quickly that sheet metal was very sharp and needed to be respected, kind of like women.

It was time to grow so Mike hired a guy that was very knowledgeable about air-conditioning and heating. We started taking on new construction work and the company was growing well. I did what I knew best and that was in the sales, service, and installation of evaporative coolers. I ran the sheet-metal and fabrication aspects of the company and even started designing ductwork for the new construction division of the company. They kept me so busy I never got involved with the service and repair of air-conditioning and heating, all I knew was evaporative cooling and sheet-metal. A couple of years down the road, Mike decided it was time to move on to something else. He offered the company to me and I said "You know I don't really have the money to buy your company so I'll just work for whoever buys it." He eventually sold it to some people that were working for Mike at the time. I thought to myself, "Why am I going to go to work for them, when I know more than they do about running a company. You know what, I'm going to step away and start my own evaporative cooling company." We named the company Desert Cooler Specialist.

I started Desert Cooler Specialist in 1986 with just one truck operating out of my garage, and with no customers. I went around and left flyers at homes and advertised in a little weekly mobile home newspaper. At the time there were probably 15 or 20 mobile home parks and that little weekly newspaper is where I got my first customers. We got quite a bit of business in 1986, our first year. I think we did a little over $23,000 in revenue ($49,557 in 2014 dollars). Things were a little hectic in the beginning. My family was growing, we now had two boys and my wife was working in the super market. I would work in the evaporative cooling business during the day and was a waiter at night in a local restaurant to help support my family. I've always had this entrepreneurial spirit of being in control of my own destiny. As a waiter I was in control of how much money I could make each night. I learned early on that if I could give my customers a dining experience instead of just throwing food at them, I could make great money. It was all about customer service and exceeding their expectation. I've always had a passion for helping others get what they want. When I was very young – eight or nine years old – I would tie our lawnmower behind my bicycle and go around the neighborhood mowing lawns to make some extra money. In my twenty's, Mike and I were involved in several small oddball entrepreneurial businesses such as diving for golf balls and boat bottom cleaning.

Some of the clients I have today will occasionally come up to me and say, "You know, I remember when you used to come to my house with Mickey Albright to service my cooler. He treated you so bad and I felt so sorry for you." I would say to them, "Please don't. That man taught me so much. Not only did he teach me about evaporative cooling but also about taking care of the client and doing the right thing." That's our whole motto, take care of the client first and then take care of the equipment. Almost 30 years later my passion has not changed, and that's why our business card reads: "Your Comfort...Our Passion".

I hope you find this book informative and it helps you understand how evaporative cooling can improve your life style, your health and reduce your utilities during the hot summer months.

Buff Brown is available for speaking engagements, Radio and TV interviews, education & consulting at:

http://www.desertcoolerspecialist.com

(760) 832-8737

info@desertcoolerspecialist.com

Why I Chose Evaporative Cooling as a Career?

I think evaporative cooling chose me in a way. While I worked for Mike and his company I was running everything on the evaporative cooling and sheet metal sides of the business. I didn't have the time to learn anything else. Nobody said, "Come on let me teach you about air conditioning." I just focused on evaporative cooling and sheet metal.

Back in the '60's and '70's, evaporative cooling became very, very popular because of how cheap it was to operate and the comfort it provided. Evaporative cooling was very inexpensive to install and service back then. If you had air-conditioning in your house, you were in the upper income echelon; up at the country club level. Most of the mobile homes and the lower/middle income people used evaporative cooling during the summer as the only way to stay cool. Back in the early '60's and '70's during the summer – June, July and August – Palm Springs pretty much became a ghost town because of how hot it would get. Virtually everybody would leave the desert and go somewhere cooler. My family would go to San Diego for three

1

months to avoid the heat. Not a lot of people hung out in Palm Springs during the summer, but those that did had swamp coolers.

I think what I like most about swamp coolers and evaporative cooling is they have few moving parts and you don't need to be a rocket scientist to work on them. Coolers cost a lot less to service and install compared to central air-conditioning. Additionally, air-conditioning companies in the valley really did not like to work on, install, service or sell evaporative coolers. I remember thinking to myself, "There's a niche here and people need somebody to take care of that professionally".

Because most air-conditioning companies did not want to work on swamp coolers, they often did terrible, shoddy work where they overcharged the customer and rarely fixed the issue. I would get so frustrated when a client would call me up after some other company had worked on their evaporative cooler and it still was not cooling. Frequently, I would arrive at the equipment and just stand there shaking my head.

True Story: I once went to one job where the client had called an air-conditioning company and the technician didn't have any cooler filter media, but he did have air-conditioning filter media on his truck. Guess what I found? Instead of using factory recommended Aspen Pad filter media, he cut air conditioning filter media called "hog hair" from a roll and put it in the filter racks and charged the customer. "Hog hair" filter media has no cooling capacity; it's a filter designed to catch debris from getting into your air-conditioning system, there is no way it will cool. I couldn't believe that a company would allow their technician to do something like that and take advantage of a homeowner.

Hog-Hair filters in cooler

I've always had a passion for helping people and doing what's right for them. I was seeing a lot of customers being taken advantage of in the servicing and installation of their evaporative cooling systems. Like anything else, if you don't like doing it, you won't do it well and if you don't do the job correctly, it's not going to work to the manufacturer's specifications. I think evaporative cooling more or less picked me. We both came to an agreement: "Look, I'll take care of you, you take care of me", and so far it's been a great relationship.

Notes:

_____

_____

_____

_____

_____

_____

_____

_____

_____

_____

_____

~ Chapter #1 ~

History of

Evaporative/Swamp Coolers

Evaporative cooling has been around for thousands of years despite people thinking it's only been around for 30 or 40 years. Evaporative cooling actually goes back to ancient times when the Egyptians would hang tapestry in front of palace windows and doors and would run water down the tapestries. When the afternoon breeze blew through these tapestries, it would cause a cooling effect. It could have decreased the inside temperature by as much as 10 to 15 degrees. Those Egyptians were pretty cool guys.

As the Egyptians started using this form of cooling it became very popular and spread quickly throughout the whole region. Now not only Pharaohs and Kings were enjoying this luxury, but villages were adopting this form of cooling and would drape cloths over doors and windows to stay cool.

I have heard stories of back in the very early years of Palm Springs that the old-timers would run water down burlap sacks to cool their shacks by utilizing the afternoon breeze. Keep in mind, back in those days Palm Springs was a desert oasis and there were no golf courses. It was not uncommon for the desert heat to reach 115, 120, 125 degrees. Any relief from the heat by any means possible was always welcomed.

The old timers got very innovative and started coming up with other ways of running water down a cooling media. They would put a fan in front of a moistened burlap sack to blow the air through it instead of waiting for that afternoon breeze. As long as they had electricity they could now cool down their homes at all times. Along came a company called Arctic Circle who started manufacturing what I believe was the very first basic swamp cooler.

Basic swamp coolers consist of a metal cabinet with a blower in it that's driven by a motor connected to a belt. The pan on the bottom was the water reservoir and it had some kind of pumping system that would pump water over the pads. The outside filter racks would have some type of filter media in it.

They found that Aspen wood was a great cooling media; it saturated well and held the moisture in, thus giving a larger cooling temperature range. By installing these systems on roofs or on the side of the house, they could cool the entire home and get up to 20 degrees temperature reduction during the summer!

In early 1970, a company called Arvin came to Mickey's company in a motor home that had been gutted and transformed into a showroom on wheels. They came to us in Palm Springs because we were the only swamp cooling company in the Coachella Valley and said, "Look we have this new evaporative cooler and we want to give you one to put on your shop to test out how it works."

We looked at this thing like it was something from outer space. It looked nothing like a swamp cooler as we knew them. It only had one opening and we quickly said, "This is not going to work. You're not going to get enough air flow through this one opening. You need more openings and more filter area." The filter media was made out of a cardboard-type substance. Now instead of it being one inch thick it was eight inches thick. We just thought there is no way this is going to work. One inlet, one pad, eight inches instead of one; how could this thing cool anything? You're going to need a bigger motor to pull the air through that thick pad.

They eventually convinced us this was the evaporative cooler of the future and we thought, all right, we'll go ahead and put one of these new evaporative cooling systems on our shop and see what happens.

That's when the transformation took place from the basic swamp cooler to what's now called the single-inlet system or evaporative cooler. It was revolutionary. Not only cooling much quicker and much faster with an even bigger temperature drop, but the air was also much drier. It didn't have that "swampy" feeling, especially on those mildly humid days. We were the first company in the Palm Springs area to start offering what was then called Mastercool Evaporative Cooler.

Once the Mastercool cooler caught on, it spread like wildfire. The single-inlet cooler is now today, the most efficient evaporative cooling system on the market. At the time, Mastercool was the leader in the industry of evaporative cooling. They came out with what was called a second stage unit that added a pre-cooler to the main system dropping the temperature even more.

You were able to get almost 30, 35, and sometimes 40 degree temperature difference between outside temperature and inside discharge through anywhere from 16 to 24 inches of filter media. All of a sudden, the evaporative cooling business became very popular. It was still a lot cheaper than central air conditioning to install and they were a lot cheaper to operate than air conditioning.

Mastercool went out of business in 2006 because of their poor customer service and the relocation of their manufacturing to Mexico. There was another company in Phoenix, Arizona called Phoenix Manufacturing, who was right on the heels of Mastercool in their design and concept.

When Mastercool went out of business, Phoenix Manufacturing picked up the market share and ran with it. They are now the leader in evaporative cooling manufacturing. They upgraded the system from the standard 8-inch model to their high-performance 12-inch model and their Aerocool Pro-Series, with a 4x4 filter media. It is an interesting concept in itself; with two 4-inch thick filters.

The outside filter media is a much denser filter media than your standard filter media which is backed up with a standard 4-inch filter media. It does the same thing as the 12-inch filter media, slowing down the air going through that filter media. The thicker the pad, the longer air travels through the filter media, the colder and drier the air becomes.

Today, they make commercial-size units that can cool warehouses. We recently installed six commercial-sized units that have two dual-inlets for Mercedes-Benz of Palm Springs. This means they have two 12-inch filter media on each side, and the heart that drives the blower is a 7.5 horsepower motor. During the hot summer days you can go into the automotive bay where the mechanics work and it will be anywhere from 75 to 85 degrees. And that's during the hot days in August.

Evaporative cooling has come a long way. It's much cheaper for a commercial application to run evaporative cooling than it would be to run air conditioning. Mercedes-Benz would have needed probably 50 tons of air to cool their operation and we were able to do it with 6 units which cost them a lot less to operate.

Evaporative cooling is evolving as we speak. Phoenix Manufacturing is still coming out with new products all the time. Today, they are thermostatically controlled with dual-speed operation. The thermostats can change the speed from high to low, and low to high, depending on what you set the thermostat at.

Evaporative cooling, like air conditioning, is changing very rapidly. But, it's still very basic. Evaporative coolers are very economical to operate and a third of the cost of central air conditioning to install. Evaporative cooling is here to stay. It's been around for thousands of years and I don't see it going away any time soon.

Notes:

~ Chapter #2 ~

What Should I Look for in an Evaporative Cooler?

A lot of people will call, and say, "I'm interested in getting an evaporative cooler." I'll respond, "Great. What's the square footage of your house?" They'll tell me the square footage of their house, but in their mind, they've already made a decision. They've already been to the Big Box Stores and seen this big, huge, giant evaporative cooler on the floor for $600. That's the one they want and that's what they think it's going to cost to put an evaporative cooler in their home.

This is what I tell them, "Great. What I need to do is come do a home evaluation to see exactly what the home needs and if there is a place we can install the evaporative cooler?" Not every home, believe it or not, is capable of accepting an evaporative cooling system. Because every home is different, so is every installation.

Every year, when I go out, I'll probably run into 5 to 10 homes that cannot have an evaporative cooling system. What we are looking for is, "can we do it in a ducted system? Can we do a wall-mounted system? Are they in an association, do they have a tiled roof or is there room on the side yard?" Sometimes there's just no place to put an evaporative cooling system.

First, I need to find out what your needs are. Any contractor or Big Box Store that quotes you a price without seeing you and your home is doing you a disservice. The other key elements are the Four Factors that will determine whether you want an evaporative cooler or not.

Here are the Four Factors. Two of them you have a choice on and two of them you don't.

- The Technical Requirement - You don't have a choice here. Sorry! The size of the home, the construction type, floor plan and lay out of the home will determine what size of system you need.

- Code Requirement – You don't have a choice here either. Safety and building codes, city permits. When we talk about Code requirement we are talking about the safety of your home and family.

- Environmental Choices – Your Choice. Energy efficiency – Aspen vs rigid media. Comfort enhancing options. Convenience in operation and maintenance.

- People's Choices – Your Choice of installer. Consider Commitment to Excellence, Expertise in their field, online reviews, who you trust and like.

These are the Four Factors. Two choices you don't have and two choices you do. It's just the way it is. The home determines what size of evaporative cooler is needed to keep you comfortable. Anybody can install a big evaporative cooler in the house and blow small children out the door. That's not comfort.

We design systems so that 75 percent of the time, you're running your evaporative cooler on low speed to keep the house anywhere between 76° and 82°. That's what comfort is all about.

That's why we come out and determine exactly what the square footage is, where the system can go and what type of system you want within your budget. This is why we offer you options to make sure you have the right system for your needs.

Do you want a basic swamp cooler? Or are you looking for a whole house ducted system that's ducted into all the bedrooms and the living space so the whole house is being cooled evenly? Do you want automatic relief systems to vent your unit? Are you looking for a thermostat? Or would a timer work better for you? Are you looking to cool your garage; to keep your car and garage from getting 120 degrees during the summer months? There is a lot to consider when installing an evaporative cooler. We just don't come in and say, "We're going to put an evaporative cooler in your wall and you're good to go."

We look at the whole house. That is why we ask a lot of questions when we come to your home. What kind of system are you looking for? Most of the time, people have done some research. They've gone to the Big Box Stores and looked at the units on the floor or gone to our website. Checked out other websites and done a little research. They may have even gone to a friend's house that has an evaporative cooler. Asking a lot of questions gives us insight as to what your needs are and what you can afford.

True story: We had a customer that wanted an evaporative cooler installed in his house. During the investigation with the homeowner, we asked him, "So you're here year round, right?" He says "Well no, we want this evaporative cooler so when we are gone for three months during the summer; we can have this cooler on to keep the house cool so, we don't have to run the air conditioner."

I said, "Great idea. You know, I can keep the house, even in August, at 82° to 88°. Instead of setting your air conditioner at 90° and having it cost you big dollars we can do it for pennies." I also said, "Great. Let's put it on a timer." The reason I suggested the timer is because we don't want the cooler running 24-7 and we want a drying out period. We don't need to run the cooler at night. The desert cools down. He said, "No, no, no. I want the cooler on a thermostat." I said, "Okay.

We can do that but, here's what we have found: there are certain times of the season, such as when it's hot and humid, the thermostat may not get satisfied and therefore run 24-7." He said, "That's what I want. I want that so that if it needs to run 24-7, it runs 24-7." I said, "Okay, but I don't recommend it." Ultimately the final decision is up to the client and what they want. Besides, isn't the customer always right?

We went ahead and put the unit in, in the early part of summer. I got a call in September when they got back, he said, "You need to come over here because we have a real problem." I said, "All right I'll be right there." When I walk in the house I could smell the mold. Their kitchen and living room was full of mold because their evaporative cooler had been running all summer, 24-7, especially during August and parts of September.

The cooler ran 24/7 without having a drying out period, which is what I recommended by using a timer. They had a real problem. It's very important that we find out exactly what your needs are and design the system around those needs.

Factor number one is the house is going to tell us exactly what you need and we go from there. Factor number two is a very important factor. As a licensed contractor, we follow all the city and state codes. There are certain things that need to be done to code, not only to protect us as contractors, but to protect your home and your family.

We make sure that the wiring and the water hookup is all done to code. The two basic things are, it uses electricity and it uses water. You want to make sure that it's on a separate circuit. You also want to make sure you're hooking it up to a water source that the homeowner can get to; if something should go wrong the water can be turned off.

It needs to be done with refrigerant copper for the water supply line, not with cheap copper that you would buy at Home Depot or a big box store. Code compliance and finding out exactly what the home is going to require are two important factors.

The third factor is the type of company that you're going to have installing your evaporative cooling system. You know the best source of finding out which company to use is by looking at referrals.

Today, with the Internet being as powerful as it is, going on and checking reviews; it is a great way to find out who is good at what they do and who is not so good. If I was having a heart attack, I wouldn't go to my GP for heart surgery. If I was going to put an evaporative cooler in, I wouldn't personally go to an air-conditioning company. Air-conditioning companies are great and we need them, but they are specialists in heating and air-conditioning.

Evaporative cooling is designed completely different, sized different, and ducted different than central air-conditioning systems. Just make sure the company that you're choosing has good references, good reviews, is knowledgeable on the equipment they are offering for your home, and backs up their work with warranties or guarantees.

The fourth and, I think, the most important factor is, the people that are going to install your system.

You know, a lot of times I get clients that say, "Yes, we want to go ahead and have you install our cooling system."

"I have one question for you though. And that question is; are the guys that are showing up – do any of them speak English?" I look at them and I kind of shake my head, "You know, fortunately sir, all of them do." "Oh well that's a relief."

As a business owner, I want my employees to be able to communicate with the homeowner exactly what they are going to do when they get there. Introduce themselves and introduce their team. Then put down floor runners and carpet runners to protect your home.

When they are done, they walk the customer through the system showing them how to operate the controls, as well as how to work the windows in conjunction with their evaporative cooler.

You also want to make sure the company is going to send out installers and technicians that have been background checked and drug tested.

There are a lot of strange characters in today's society. Did you know the number one trade taught in the prison system today is plumbing, and air-conditioning is number two? I have another true story for you on that.

When I had an air-conditioning company, a technician comes in for an interview. He had impeccable credentials, EPA certified, and current on all the new refrigerants. However, on the application we have a place that reads, "Have you ever been convicted of a felony?" The applicant wrote on there "will explain". I got down to that part of the application and said, "What can you tell me about this answer you indicated "will explain"?

Have you ever been charged with a felony?" He said, "Well, yes. I'll tell you about that." Turns out he was at a bar, got in a fight, pulled a knife on a guy and stabbed him. That technician sitting across from me, the guy who pulled out the knife ended up going to prison. I looked him in the eye and said, "As you should have gone to prison.

You have great credentials. Unfortunately, you're not the team member we are looking for." I don't know where he ended up, but those technicians are out there.

The Four Factors are something that a lot of companies don't know about and a lot of homeowners don't look at. We feel that as your comfort specialist these factors are what govern our integrity, and we always follow it to the letter to protect you and your family.

Making sure you are comfortable and to make sure the job is done the way it should be done.

Notes:

_____

_____

_____

_____

_____

_____

_____

_____

_____

_____

What Type of Environment is Best for Evaporative Cooling?

Because evaporative cooling works hand-in-hand with Mother Nature there are certain conditions that are great for evaporative coolers and there are conditions evaporative coolers don't work at all. Evaporative coolers work best in a dry and hot climate, like here in the southern California desert, Phoenix, Arizona, Utah, Colorado and New Mexico.

In these areas, evaporative cooling is very, very popular because of the hot, dry climates. An evaporative cooler would be useless in Florida because of the high humidity. They work best when it's hot and dry; "hot" means anywhere from 80° to 115°. Once it starts getting past 115° though, like 118°or 120°, you're pushing the envelope. It is unlikely an evaporative cooler will be able to perform better than keeping your home cooler than 84° to 86°.

Now that range could be comfortable to some people, but it's not comfortable to me. Everybody is different when it comes to evaporative cooling. What I like in evaporative cooling, and what you like in evaporative cooling, could vary anywhere from 5° to 15°.

True story: When we go back in the fall to do our winter close down on evaporative coolers, I like to check with new clients who had a system installed and ask them, "How did it work, did it keep you comfortable, what did it do for your utility bills?" Undoubtedly, these people will tell me, "You know what? We did not turn on our air conditioner once this summer."

Knowing what kind of summer we had, and knowing that there were certain times in August and September that it was pretty doggone humid. I find myself thinking these people are very, very brave and their comfort level must be a lot higher than mine. Or maybe they only ran their air-conditioners a couple of days. It's fun to find out the different comfort levels people have. "What is your comfort zone?"

I get calls from all around the world because of our website and because people want to know about evaporative cooling. The other day I received a call from New York City. I thought, "Oh it's probably a stockbroker trying to sell stocks from New York City." I took the call. "Hello. This is Buff." There was a silence on the other end of the line. He said, "Yes, is this the Desert Cooler Specialist?"

I said, "Yes, this is Buff with Desert Cooler Specialist. How can I make your day?" He said, "Oh great, I've been looking at your website and I need some information on evaporative cooling. We're going to be building a greenhouse and I want to know, will evaporative cooling work in my greenhouse?" I said, "Great, can I ask you a question? What city are you located in?" He said, "We are in Manhattan." I exclaimed, "Wow! All right, well this is a new one."

I began asking questions. That's what I do. I ask a lot of questions. "First of all, what type of greenhouse is this going to be for? What are you going to be growing in it? How big is your greenhouse going to be? What's the square footage? And what's the height of the ceilings?

Whereabouts in Manhattan are you putting this greenhouse?" He said, "Well you've asked some very interesting questions."

First of all, we're going to be building this greenhouse on the roof of a high-rise building in downtown Manhattan." That makes sense because there's no place in Manhattan other than the roof of a skyscraper to put a greenhouse. I said, "All right. What is the temperature there in Manhattan during the summer?" He said, "Well up on this roof it can get very hot. It can get to 110°, 115°."

I said, "Really, I didn't think Manhattan got that hot." He said, "Well, normally in downtown Manhattan it will be 98° to 105°, but it will be very humid." I said, "Okay, now we're getting some solid information here. What's the humidity usually in Manhattan during the summer?" "Oh," he said "it could be as high as 50, 60, sometimes70 percent."

I said, "Okay, well evaporative coolers usually work best in dry climates." He said, "Again, we're building this on a roof and if you're up there for more than an hour, it's like you're going to have a heat stroke." I started thinking, and said, "You know what? On top of this roof, is the building that you're setting the greenhouse on surrounded by other buildings?" He replied, "Oh yes, you know Manhattan, we have skyscrapers with a lot of glass acting like mirrors." "Okay, now we're getting someplace.

So you've got this greenhouse you're going to build on top of a roof in Manhattan. And it is surrounded by other skyscrapers that have a lot of glass, that are acting like a magnifying glass on the roof. And you're telling me that it can be anywhere from 110° to 115°." I tell him to take temperature and humidity readings on the roof for the next two weeks and get back to me. That will give us a better idea of what type of system you can use.

True Story: I once went into a house that was maybe 1200 square feet. The gentleman came out and told me exactly what he wanted. "I want a 6500 CFM with a 1 horsepower motor into one opening." I said "That sounds great. So let me ask you a question. Do you have any dogs or kids?

"Yeah, I have two dogs and three kids." "Great". When you turn the cooler on and open the front door, do you want to blow them out of the house when it comes on?" He says, "What do you mean?" Bigger is not necessarily better when it comes to evaporative cooling. A 6500 CFM cooler in a house this size, with a single opening, is much more than you need. There is a noise factor and there's a volume factor. We want to design a system that's best for you, your home and family. That's why we need to come out and do a complete evaluation of the home to make sure that we are giving you the best system for your home and your family.

Notes:

_____

_____

_____

_____

_____

_____

_____

_____

_____

_____

~ Chapter #4 ~

How Much Money Can I Really Save with an Evaporative Cooler?

Every time I get a call from people that are interested in putting in evaporative cooling, my first question to them is, "Why?" Their answer back to me, undoubtedly, 99.9 percent of the time is, "I want to save on my utilities."

Well, evaporative cooling – according to Southern California Edison – could save up to 75 percent off your utility bill by installing an evaporative cooling system. Depending on what your comfort zone is, everybody's percentage savings is going to be different.

In the Palm Springs region of California, by February or March it starts to warm up outside. And by warm-up, I'm talking 80° – 95°. Many people look for cooling relief by using Mother Nature's most efficient means of cooling. Some say they are cooling the green way with evaporative coolers.

Instead of running and turning on your air-conditioner in February, a lot of people enjoy spending pennies on the dollar to keep their house at a comfortable 74° – 78°.

Why does it cost pennies compared to air-conditioning? Nine out of ten evaporative coolers have a 120 volt system. There is a motor and a pump. The total amp draw is going to be anywhere from 12 to 18 amps.

Now let's look at why an air conditioner costs <u>much</u> more to operate. An air conditioner has a lot of moving parts. If you have a split system, which most homes do, you have two pieces of equipment, an outside unit and an inside unit.

The inside unit has a blower motor. The blower motor is usually a 120 volt system and usually uses around 8 to 12 running amps. We are not done adding up the amp draw yet, keep reading.

Outside, you have the condensing unit that has two major parts in it. The part on top, the condensing fan motor, is what you see spinning around and discharging the hot air from the housing. It usually has a 230 volt motor. The amperage draw, depending on the size of the motor, is probably going to be from 10 to 12 amps. Now the heart of the system is your compressor. That's where your biggest load comes from.

On an old system – a 10 to 12 year old system – the startup amps – in other words, the amount of energy it takes to start the compressor – could be as much as 24 to 28 amps.

Once it gets going, it'll drop down, but it's still going to be running at a very, very high-end. Don't forget your air conditioner cycles on and off, so the next time it starts up you have a spike in amps, again and again. I'll let you add all those amps up. Amps are what cost you money.

On very high efficient air conditioners with a two-stage compressor, two-stage condensing fan motors and variable speed blower motors, the operating cost could be as much, or less than an evaporative cooler.

So why should you install an evaporative cooler when you can go with a very high efficiency air conditioner and it could be more energy efficient than an evaporative cooler? Here are a few reasons.

Air-conditioning is designed to extract all the moisture out of your house. That means your furniture, the walls and you. Many times I've heard people complain to me they are running a humidifier to add moisture into the house because they wake up in the morning with a bloody nose due to the air-conditioner drying out their sinuses.

In fact, a properly designed system should actually cycle on and off. This can be somewhat annoying depending on how the system was designed. It will come on, cool down, and shut off. Five minutes later after the house warms, it'll kick back on. The lights may dim a little from the power draw it requires to start up. It will cool down and then shut back off. And that goes on and on and on.

Sound familiar? That's why your utility bill continues to climb higher and higher and higher.

It's not uncommon for us to go into a home and have people tell us that they have utility bills of $300, $400, $600, even $1,200 a month while keeping their thermostat at 78° to 82°, and they are miserable. In fact, they are so frustrated with their living conditions they are contemplating leaving the Palm Springs area.

They're thinking about moving out of the state because of high utility bills. I tell them, "That's definitely an option. It sounds like an expensive option, but there's another way. And this is what we can do."

The real benefit to evaporative cooling that is even greater than the utility saving is the comfort it provides. I'm sure you've been to the beach on a hot day, but still found yourself very comfortable because the waves were crashing on the beach and occasionally there was some spray from the ocean.

That cool breeze wasn't just a cool breeze. There was moisture in the breeze that felt extra refreshing to you. Or, have you ever been around a waterfall and felt that cool, moist breeze against your skin? Evaporative cooling works on the same concept.

During the summer your body perspires and works as your internal air-conditioning system. The hotter it gets, the more we perspire to keep down our body temperature. If you ever find that you have stopped perspiring during the summertime, be aware, you are now close to having a heat stroke. It's a natural reaction for your body to perspire.

With evaporative cooling, we're changing the air in the home every 2 to 3 minutes with clean, fresh, healthy, moisturized air. What this does is bring in clean fresh, healthy air and it pushes out all the old, hot, stale air. With central air conditioning – you just recycle the same existing stale air in the house over and over and over.

I'm sure you've heard of people during the summer that get a summer cold. Perhaps your child comes home from school with the sniffles and then within three days, boom, the child's sick. Within two or three more days, the other kids come down with it. Before long, guess who else comes down with the sniffles? Most likely mom or dad is next. Then before you know it, the whole family is sick.

The reason is that when they sneeze, particulates are expelled from their mouth into the air. The air-conditioning system picks it up and cycles it through your house. I hear people say, "You know, I've had this cold for a month." Yeah, it's because you got it when you came home. Your home is recycling the same sick air over and over.

Another nice thing I like about evaporative cooling is the system can run 24/7. We typically start our system up in February and run it through June, sometimes through parts of July, even parts of August, and then into September. We definitely run it in October. In fact, there have been times, in the Palm Springs area on Christmas day it has been 85° and we'll kick on the evaporative cooler to circulate some fresh air throughout the house.

Another nice thing about evaporative cooling is that it runs constantly to keep your home with a consistent pleasant, fresh cool feeling. There is no cycling on and off during the day, like with an air conditioner. You are waiting for the house to warm so the system can cycle back on again to cool you.

We set the thermostat at what we are comfortable with, which is usually the low setting on the thermostat, and we constantly experience a cool waterfall like breeze going throughout the home. We're able to open up doors and windows. Parents love the fact that they don't have to yell at the kids, "Close the door, the air-conditioner is on!" when they use the pool.

We get to open up the house and bring nature in. Adding moisture to the home and the air we breathe during the hot, dry months. Also we're not waking up all dried out or with a bloody nose. Many people comment that they sleep much better with evaporative cooling than they do with air-conditioning.

In fact, during the latter part of the season, like October and November, we still run the evaporative cooler. In the summer when house guests arrive my wife will say, "Uh-oh, here's an extra blanket. It's going to snow in the house tonight. Buff is turning on the cooler." We love sleeping under blankets in the summer, all snuggly in our beds.

There are so many uses for evaporative cooling. Like when we want to sit out on the patio in the afternoon; we turn the evaporative cooler on high, close all the doors and windows except the one that goes out to the patio, and all that cool, refreshing air is forced out through the door, keeping us cool while we enjoy the sunset.

Notes:

_____

_____

_____

_____

_____

_____

_____

_____

_____

_____

_____

_____

_____

_____

_____

_____

_____

_____

Is The Big Box Store the Best Place to Buy an Evaporative Cooler?

In my opinion, the big box stores such as Home Depot, Lowe's, Ace Hardware, etc., are all great stores to go to for home improvement. The nice thing about those big-box stores is they have a great return policy. I even shop there.

However, if I need a plumber, like when I recently had a leak under my foundation slab, I called a plumber. I didn't run to Home Depot and say, "Look I need a jackhammer. I need this and that. I have a leak in my slab." No, I called a professional.

The big-box stores during the spring and summer season sell an evaporative cooler line made by Champion which has the Mastercool logo on it. In my opinion, it is nowhere near to the quality of the original Mastercool cooler. But that's what they offer and people assume it is the same, high quality Mastercool unit they are familiar with from years past. A lot of people go in, look at these coolers and then call a guy over in an orange apron.

"Hey, I have some questions on this evaporative cooler. I'm thinking about putting an evaporative cooler on my house. What size cooler should I go with?" The guy in the orange apron could be from plumbing, lumber, the door hanging department or some other department.

Undoubtedly, he is probably going to either get you somebody that's familiar with this department or he may say, "I put one of these coolers on my house and I got this great big cooler right here. It is awesome. It keeps my house at 76°. It's amazing. Get this cooler here. It's a great cooler."

The homeowner thinks, "That's got to be the cooler for me." And he decides, "Yeah, go ahead and write me up". They'll load him up and away he goes. As the homeowner gets home he finally thinks, "But wait, how am I going to install this?"

The homeowner starts calling around to contractors. We get a lot of calls from people saying, "Hey, I bought a cooler at Home Depot and I need somebody to install it. Will you install it?" Nine times out of ten we will not. It's a liability issue with us. Nine times out of ten we find the homeowner purchased the wrong cooler.

But remember, the reason they bought it was the guy in the orange apron said, "Yeah, this cooler will work." If it doesn't work – and this is his closing line – "If it doesn't work, bring it on back. We'll exchange it for anything." Great, now you get to lug that huge box back to the store, stand in line again, and hope to get the correct unit.

That's the one thing about the big-box stores, they have a great return policy but you know what? If I'm going to go into a project that has to do with my comfort and cooling my home I want to make sure I'm going to be doing the right thing with the right equipment and the right people to install it.

True story: I once had a customer call up and say, "I just had this cooler installed by someone else about a month ago and it's not working. Can you come over and look at it?" Absolutely! We will be more than happy to. We pull up to the house, look up on the roof and immediately know exactly what has happened. On the roof sits one of the big-box store coolers. So, like we always do, we started asking questions.

Especially on a job like this, I often ask the homeowner to tell me why I'm there. Usually when I ask "why am I here", the homeowner opens up and tells me every reason that I'm there. What's happened, what's going on, the problems they've had, who did the install, why exactly they called me out?

I gather information and say, "Great, let us go up and take a look to see what's going on." As my assistant and I climb on the roof our suspicions are confirmed and sure enough it's one of the big-box store Champion coolers. As a licensed contractor the first thing we start looking at is if the system is installed properly and up to code, for you and your homes safety.

After our evaluation, we went down to talk to the homeowner and asked more questions.

"So tell me about the people that installed your unit?" "Well, my old cooler was rusted out. I called the home warranty people and they sent out two guys. They looked at it and said, 'Yeah, we can install it, and we'll go get the cooler.'"

Well, the home warranty company went to the big-box store, picked up the wrong cooler, came back and installed it. These guys were handymen, at best.

The homeowner's electric bill had actually tripled since he had the new evaporative cooler installed. This particular system was tied into his air-conditioning duct system. In some older homes, tying the evaporative cooling into the central air-conditioning system is a possibility if the home has old style galvanized ductwork.

Galvanized ductwork is much larger and can take the volume of air that an evaporative cooler puts out. However, there's one necessary component these glorified handymen didn't install in his cooler; an automatic backdrop damper system at the unit.

Since it was installed in conjunction with his central air-conditioning system, every time he ran his air-conditioning at least 50 percent of his air-conditioning went out the cooler and he was actively cooling off Palm Springs.

No wonder his utility bill was three times more than it should have been! We found many more problems. It was not hooked up properly, the low speed was on high, the high speed was on low, the electrical work wasn't to code and the water line was dripping on the roof.

What a shame, this cooler was only a month old. The customer had to endure the inconvenience of higher electric bills because the home warranty company sent out inexperienced technicians who really had no clue what they were doing.

What I'm saying is 9 times out of 10 when you go to a big box store and buy a cooler you're not going to get the whole package. They are not going to tell you that you need a thermostat package, or how to operate the cooler, or that you are going to need a motor.

The coolers at the big-box stores do not come with a motor. You have to install a motor, water line, electrical, etc. What size motor do you need for each particular cooler? Does the cooler require an auto flush out system which flushes the water from the cooler every four to eight hours so that your filter media will last 4 to 6 years longer? Is it being tied into a duct system? Is it being installed into a wall?

Is the electrical up to code? What about your water supply line? There are a lot of things that they are not going to tell you because they probably don't know. It's like calling up a doctor and saying, "Doctor, I don't feel good. I ache and I have a runny nose. Can you write me a prescription?" Ninety percent chance your doctor is going to say, "You know what?

You need to come to the office. I need to examine you, I need to ask you questions, and at that time, I will determine the proper treatment for your symptoms." That's what needs to be done when you're thinking about installing an evaporative cooler in your home.

You need to have the right people come out to determine exactly what type of system you need and what's going to be required to make the system operate properly. Most importantly, we need to determine what's going to keep you and your family safe and comfortable once that system is installed.

Notes:

_____

_____

_____

_____

_____

_____

_____

_____

_____

_____

_____

_____

_____

_____

~ Chapter #6 ~

Can I Have Both an Evaporative Cooler and Air Conditioner in My Home?

A lot of times people will call and say, "I'm thinking about replacing our central air conditioner with a high-efficiency air-conditioning system." I'll enthusiastically say, "That's great. It will really reduce your utilities and increase your comfort." And she replies, "Well, the only reason that we are contemplating not doing that is because we're looking at evaporative cooling instead. We are not sure that we can have both."

My question is, "Why are you thinking about evaporative cooling? What is driving you in that direction?" She replies, "When we run the air conditioner during the day we have it at 78 to 82 degrees, and at night we really can't sleep with those temperatures. We lower it to 76 degrees at night so we can sleep. Every time we wake up in the morning, my husband's nose is all dried out; often he gets a bloody nose. I haven't slept well. We're thinking of an alternative of maybe putting a humidifier in that room to add moisture, but that means the air-conditioner is never going to shut off because it's trying to extract the moisture from the house."

I said, "You know, a lot of people have both systems in their home. They have both evaporative cooling and central air-conditioning. It's what we've coined "the dual cool system". Meaning you have the option of either using your evaporative cooler or your central air conditioning depending on what the weather conditions are outside and what your comfort level is.

The dual cool system does not combine the evaporative cooling system with your central air-conditioning system. The reason that you don't do that is central air-conditioning is designed for much smaller volume of air than evaporative cooling. If you look around your house you'll notice that the ducts are not that big. For air-conditioning system duct in bathrooms, for instance, we'll run a small five inch duct. Into a bedroom we'll run a seven inch duct and into a living room an eight inch duct. With an evaporative cooler we will run anywhere from a ten inch to a fourteen inch duct for the largest rooms in the house for maximum airflow.

The volume of air that evaporative cooling puts out is twice as much as central air-conditioning.

You can't take something that's designed to move a lot of air and stick it into duct system that's designed to move only a little bit of air, such as air conditioning. You'll hear a whistling noise; due of the restricted size of the duct system airflow. This can cause expensive motors to burn out more frequently. These are two totally different systems. They both move air, but each move air in different ways. With air-conditioning we close up the house. Including all the doors, windows, and the drapes and we sit in a corner and watch the electrical meter spin. With evaporative cooling, it allows us to open up doors and windows to let the outdoors in and still maintain our comfort.

A dual cooling system is ideal for areas that have hot, dry climates, but you don't want to tie it into your central air-conditioning duct system. Don't get confused with dual cool systems as a combination of an air conditioning and evaporative cooling system together.

It's just a term we coined that allows you to have the option for either central air-conditioning or evaporative cooling.

Notes:

_____

_____

_____

_____

_____

_____

_____

_____

_____

_____

_____

_____

_____

_____

_____

_____

_____

_____

_____

Do I Need to Maintain my Evaporative Cooler, and if so, How Often and Why?

Your evaporative cooler works very hard to keep you and your family comfortable during the hot summer months. Just like your air-conditioning and heating system should be serviced on a regular basis and needs to be maintained twice a year – so does your evaporative cooler.

Your evaporative cooler needs to be serviced in the springtime before it is needed for cooling. That's when it's thoroughly broken down and properly cleaned. The filters are cleaned or replaced, depending on what type of filter media it has.

We always replace the water control valve and the V drive belt system because we have found over thirty years of experience, those are the two parts that usually fail the most and usually cause the most problems during the summer.

It's ironic that we take our car in to get serviced and they put a little sticker up in the left hand corner of the windshield that tells you when your next service is. We are always looking at that and comparing it to the mileage on the odometer to make sure that we don't go over it. God forbid that we should go over our miles because who knows, it may blow up or something.

We spend less time in our automobiles than we do in our homes but, we seem to neglect our home comfort systems more than our cars. Why? Taking care of your home comfort system can save you a lot of time and money in the long run.

Evaporative coolers should be serviced twice a year to insure proper cooling and to eliminate costly repairs or replacement. Your evaporative cooler works hard all summer long to keep you comfortable.

With proper maintenance of your evaporative cooler it could last 10, 12, 15 years.

But like anything else, if it's not maintained and serviced properly, it can cost you more money in repairs and utility costs; besides making you ill.

Many times the first question I ask the homeowner is: "When was the last time you had your system serviced and by whom?" Most customers tell me, "We had it serviced last year." Or, "It's been a couple of years." Or, "My air conditioning guy just serviced it a month ago".

True Story: There have been times when we arrived at a home, upon opening up the system we literally found trees or plants growing out of the wet section or the reservoir section where the water sits.

At that point it's pretty safe for me to say you probably haven't had that system serviced in more than two or three years because there's a bush growing out of the cooler!

Look at this!

What is this doing to your system? Whenever you have stagnant water in an evaporative cooler for a long period of time, you run the risk of contaminating the filter media with harmful bacteria. Think about it, this black slimy, smelly water has been sitting in your cooler for who knows how long.

It's hot out and you need some cooling in the home, so you turn on the evaporative cooler. For the first three to five minutes the pump comes on and pre-wets the filter media with water from the Black Lagoon.

As this black, smelly water flows down the filter media, contaminating it; the blower kicks in and now you are blowing all that smelly, bacteria filled air into your home.

I've had many people say, "Well, I stopped using the cooler because it was affecting my breathing. I was having allergy problems."

Evaporative coolers need to be serviced twice a year. If they use Aspen pad filters, they need to be replaced yearly. Celdek filter media; either standard or high-performance, need to be cleaned yearly and replaced every 3-5 years.

During the wintertime, we don't use our evaporative coolers. Daytime temperatures will be 50° to 70°, sometimes down into the low 30s and freezing at night. Water is not circulated with the wet section, so it needs to be properly closed down for the season. We think this is the most important service for your evaporative cooler.

If the evaporative cooler hasn't been closed down properly, the water just sits there stagnant and the filter media collects mold and mildew. It also corrodes the system. Corrosion is evaporative cooler's number one enemy. Closing down the evaporative cooler during the wintertime is the most important service because it'll help you prolong the life of your system.

Servicing your evaporative cooler is just as important as servicing your heating and air-conditioning system. You certainly service your automobile and you spend less time in that than you do in your home. Take care of your home comfort system and it'll take care of you by giving you many years of comfort.

An evaporative cooler that has not been serviced for a long period of time will actually cost you more in utility costs. If serviced properly, you may find that you can use your cooler a lot longer during the season, saving you from having to turn on your central air conditioning system.

It's like anything else. If you take care of it, it will take care of you. Make sure that you have the right company, which is familiar with evaporative coolers.

A lot of air-conditioning companies don't carry evaporative cooler parts on their trucks. Many times they will get into the middle of servicing or repairing your cooler and say, "Oh, I need to go get a pump," or "I need to go get a water control valve" or "I need to go get something."

Your time is very valuable and you want to make sure that the company you choose is very knowledgeable about evaporative coolers and that their trucks are fully stocked with evaporative cooler parts.

Notes:

_____

_____

_____

_____

_____

_____

_____

_____

What are the Different Types of Media Available for Evaporative Cooling Systems?

As you know by now, evaporative cooling goes back to ancient Egypt where the Egyptians would hang tapestry down their palace openings and have their servants run water down them. When the afternoon or evening breeze came through and blew through these tapestries, it would help cool down their palaces.

This technique was so popular that it spread throughout all of Egypt and other regions as well. Filter media has been around for a long time. Through the ages we've improved on the filter media used for evaporative cooling. I'd like to go over the different types of media and the pros and cons of different types of filter media on the market today.

One type of filter media the big box stores carry is a **Green Pliable Filter Media**. It's made out of paper.

You can either get it in pre-cut sizes or in a roll. It's not a filter media we recommend. In fact, it has the worst cooling capacity of any filter media on the market. It is paper and when paper gets wet for a long period of time it has a tendency to sag and it leaves gaps at the top of the filter racks, allowing warm air to come into the system, not giving you proper cooling.

It comes on a roll and its convenience makes it popular because it is easy to cut with a pair of scissors to fit any evaporative cooler. A lot of air-conditioning companies like to use this type of filter media because it comes in a roll and they can service almost any size evaporative cooler with it. It is convenient for them. It's not an efficient cooling media for you.

The other filter media that's on the market today is a **Synthetic Aqua Pad Filter Media**. You can get it in precut sizes or on a roll as well. Again, a lot of air-conditioning companies like to use this because of the convenience for them. This has a tendency to not wet out completely.

In other words, you'll get streaks of water running down through the filter media and it doesn't saturate the filter media completely. It's not our favorite filter media and we do not recommend it.

Now, for your basic evaporative cooler, the filter media we and the factory recommend is **Aspen Filter Media**. A lot of people say it looks like straw and it's actually Aspen wood that comes in different grades. The way you can tell if you have a really good quality Aspen filter media, is when you hold it up to the light and you can't see through it.

The nice thing about Aspen Filter Media is that it swells up twice its size. Why is that so important? Keep in mind, the thicker the pad, the colder the air.

You should always check the quality of the filter media when you purchase filter media at any of the big box store. If you hold it up and you can see through it, it's a lesser quality. At Desert Cooler Specialist, we only use factory recommended high quality Aspen filter media.

All of our service trucks carry five of the most common filter sizes which allow us to service any evaporative cooler that we come across. Now that we've talked about basic evaporative coolers and the three different filter medias that are available let's get into some high-performance systems.

About thirty years ago, a company called Mastercool came out with a design that revolutionized the evaporative cooling industry. It was a single inlet system with an eight inch filter media and the blower drew air through one single piece of media called Celdek.

What's the difference between this and, say your Aspen filter media? Well, the standard eight inch Celdek will outperform your Aspen filter media by as much as five to seven degrees with not only colder air but drier air as well. With proper maintenance this filter media can last four to six years before needing to be replaced.

Our next filter media is the high-performance, twelve inch filter media, or the 4 x 4 filter media. These filter media will outperform your basic Aspen pad coolers by as much as ten to twelve degrees and at 100 percent cooling capacity, you don't lose any efficiency. The nice thing about this filter media is with proper maintenance and twice a year service it could last anywhere from 4 to 6 years.

You're not replacing the filter media every year as you would with the Aspen pads. You'll also be able to use the system for a longer period of time and at higher temperatures to give you better comfort with better filtration for your home.

Notes:

_____

_____

_____

_____

_____

_____

_____

_____

_____

_____

_____

What Would Cause a Weird Smell or Funny Noise from my Evaporative Cooler?

There are times during the summer months when we'll get a rush of phone calls, it's usually on an overcast day when the weather is not too hot; maybe 100°, 105°. It's a dry day but we have a wind coming out of the east and people will start calling, saying "Buff, you've got to get over here, my cooler smells like fish."

There is a body of water at the end of our valley called The Salton Sea. It's very, very salty. It was very popular back in the '50's, with a yacht club and several resorts. Because the water is so salty and a limited supply of freshwater coming into it, when it gets really hot a lot of fish die.

When the winds shift, the fish die and float to the surface causing a very unpleasant, fishy smell towards the Palm Springs end of the valley. That's one scenario that we get and we just tell the customer, "Yes, that is The Salton Sea. If you'll just step outside your door, you'll notice the smell as well."

We commonly get telephone calls either late in the season or at the very beginning of the season for the same thing; a peculiar smell. It will start at the beginning of the season: March, April, May. They will call us up and say, "I just turned on my evaporative cooler and it smells swampy and very fishy."

My first question to them is "When was the last time you had your system serviced?" There is usually a silence. It's like, "Hello? Are you there?" "What do you mean serviced?" "Well, when was the last time your evaporative cooler was serviced?" "Well... I've never serviced it." "Can I ask you another question? How long have you been in the home?" "Oh, we've been in the home at least three or four years." "And you've never had your cooler serviced? That could probably be the reason."

Bacteria have formed in the filter media and in the cooler itself. Now that you've started it up and turned it on, you've stimulated the bacteria. That's why a foul smell is circulating through your home.

Later on during the summer we get what's called a monsoon season where during the day you can't run your cooler because the humidity will be too high. Many evenings the humidity will subside and you'll be able to run the cooler again.

What happens is the filter media sometimes doesn't get to dry out completely from the days' humidity and we'll get a wet zone or a semi-wet zone in the filter media.

Bacteria film starts building up in the filter media during this time. Often we will have to come out and either clean or replace the filter media due to the fact that it never got a chance to dry out. Sometimes people just run their cooler 24-7 regardless of the weather conditions and since the filter media never has an opportunity to dry out, the same bacteria can build up and cause a swampy or fishy smell.

A lot of other calls that we get: "I've got this chirping sound." Or, "I have this knocking sound." Or, "I've got this buzzing sound in my cooler. I'm sure it's nothing, but I need you to check it out." Again, my first question is, "When's the last time your system was serviced?" What we find on a lot of systems that we don't service on a regular basis is a bad V-drive belt.

Those belts, even though they are housed inside a wet environment, will dry out and will actually make a popping noise. The customer will say, "Well, no, I opened the cooler up and the noise went away, so I don't know what it is." When they open the side of the cooler the customer has created a different environment and the noise will actually stop. Any noise is a sign that something is wrong.

A lot of times what we'll find, especially on some older units such as Mastercool, is the main blower pulley has come loose. When turned on, you'll hear a click or a tick, tick, tick, tick noise. It's because the blower wheel has not been secured to the main shaft. And if you don't take care of that noise, the loose blower wheel can cause some severe damage to the cooler.

The other thing is the motor pulley which is made out of aluminum; have a setscrew that is notorious for coming loose and will cause a click, tick, tick, tick, or a rattling sound. What will happen is that the setscrew will actually score the motor shaft so bad that you can't tighten the pulley down and sometimes we have to not only replace the pulley but the entire motor as well, which is a lot pricier that regular maintenance.

Sometimes the noise could be a failing pump that's making a grinding noise. It could be a water control valve that has not been secured properly and does what we call chattering. Chattering is when air and water are in the line at the same time. The load will actually bounce the water line up and down causing a chattering sound. This sound can go through your whole house because the water supply line is connected to the plumbing lines in your home.

Again, with proper maintenance all of this can be prevented. These are things that we know to look for after 35 – 40 years of working with evaporative coolers and we know how to take care of them at the time of service. We make sure all the correct components are properly tighten. Replacing the water control valve and V-drive belt will ensure that you don't have those problems during your cooling season. We make sure the filters have been cleaned or replaced correctly.

Aspen pad filters, if not replaced on a yearly basis will start to grow purple bacteria. Keep in mind, any bacteria that form in a filter media is going to be introduced into the air stream and will eventually circulate into your home. You don't want your family breathing any bacteria and causing health problems.

Proper maintenance of the system will eliminate funny smells, strange noises and will enhance the performance of your system for that cooling season.

Notes:

_____

_____

_____

_____

_____

_____

_____

_____

What Other Benefits will I get from Owning an Evaporative Cooler Other Than Saving Money?

We get a lot of calls from people in the Palm Springs Valley for evaporative coolers, not only for their house but for warehouses and workshops. "Hey, I want to cool down my garage. You know, my garage during the summer time can get up to 120 degrees and the washer and dryer are out there. My wife hates doing laundry in the heat. You know the saying . . . happy wife, happy life? Can you help me?"

We also get a lot of calls from people that want to put evaporative coolers in their workshops, garages or man caves. Evaporative cooling is not just limited to household applications. Just this week I installed an evaporative cooler in an old bomb shelter from the '60's! True Story: I have one client that has an evaporative cooler for his three car garage. His everyday car is a new, sporty Cadillac. Next to that is a beautiful black, probably two or three year old Rolls-Royce, and next to that sits another gorgeous black Bentley that's about the same age.

He runs the evaporative cooler on a thermostat during the summer to help keep the tires from drying out, the hoses from cracking, and the leather interior from getting cracked and rough. It also keeps the wood paneling in the Bentley and the Rolls-Royce from fading. Adding moisture to the dry hot air helps keep his cars in pristine condition.

In the Palm Springs area we have hundreds of golf courses. It seems everybody, of course, has a golf cart in their garage. It's standard equipment. Like a swimming pool and a palm tree along with a 2 1/2 car garage. Yes, you guessed it; the half car garage is for your golf cart.

Many people in the desert go away for two or three months during the summer and leave their golf cart and sometimes a primary car.

During the summer, our garages in the desert can get as hot as 100°, 110°, 115°. I've seen it as high as 125° in a garage.

The garage is probably the largest source of heat gain of any home. Because you open the garage, pull in a hot car with a hot engine that's been running outside in the heat, then close the garage, it can add a large heat load to the house. That's an illustration of a huge heat gain we don't normally think about in our garage that affects your cooling system.

I once had a client tell me they came back from being away for the summer and found their nice custom-made golf cart with battery acid all over it and the garage floor. It got so hot in the garage that the batteries actually exploded.

Customers will come back after the summer and take a look at their nice car they've left and notice the leather has started to deteriorate. Also, the tires and belts need changing more often because of the heat cracking them.

They also found their utility bills– even though they have their air-conditioner inside set at 90° – still hasn't gone down. Not realizing the garage refrigerator with all the soda pops, waters, beer and wine in it has been running 24-7 because the garage is 120°.

You know, a refrigerator in an uncooled garage can increase your utilities by as much as $40-$50 per month over the course of the summer.

By installing an evaporative cooler, even on our worst days – say in August – when it's 120° outside and 70 percent humidity, we can keep the garage at 90° or below. Granted, it may not be someplace you want to go out to and tinker on your golf clubs or work in the workshop but, it's certainly going to keep the garage a lot more comfortable than 120 degrees.

It will cut down on utility costs because the heat from the garage won't transfer to the main home through the walls and the ceiling. It's going to help the refrigerator, as it won't run 24-7 to keep those beverages in there nice and cool. The cooler will cycle on and off, thus helping the refrigerator run more efficiently.

And you won't be changing the batteries in your golf cart every year.

An evaporative cooler is a great way to help reduce the heat load in a workshop, an enclosed patio and certainly in a garage. There are a lot of applications for an evaporative cooler besides just your home.

Notes:

_____

_____

_____

_____

_____

_____

_____

_____

_____

_____

_____

_____

_____

_____

_____

_____

_____

_____

~Chapter #11 ~

Frequently Asked Questions

How long will I be able to use my evaporative cooler during the summer months?

Normally we start up our coolers in February or March and can usually use it up through parts of July. August and September are normally known for air conditioning because of the high humidity that rolls into the desert. During those later summer months the cooler may be used as the humidity subsides in the evening.

Often the evenings will be cool enough that the cooler can be enjoyed throughout the night. Keep this in mind however, everybody's comfort is different and some people happily run their cooler throughout the summer.

I have some customers that never use their air conditioning and only use their evaporative cooler year round. For the most part though, you're able to use your cooler from 6 to 8 months out of the year. You can use it a lot longer than you may want to use your central air conditioning, and keep in mind, evaporative cooling costs you pennies to operate.

Air conditioning costs you dollars to operate. Your comfort is one issue and what Mother Nature dishes out is another that determines how long of a season you'll be able to use your evaporative cooler for.

Why do I need to winterize my evaporative cooler? I'd like to use it year round?

We feel that the winterizing of your evaporative cooling is one of the most important things you can do for your system. To make sure you prolong the life of your evaporative cooler follow these steps.

Winterize your evaporative cooler, shut off the water supply line and disconnect it from the shutoff valve in case it should freeze. Physically drain and properly clean out the complete system.

Clean the filter media, tank, and pumps and do any rust prevention at that time. Installing a winter cover will ensure your system stays clean during the winter months.

The reason you should do this is because you don't want stagnant water sitting in your cooler for three or four months. It can cause corrosion, rust, and possibly build up bacteria in the filter media inside your cooler.

Just because you close it down doesn't mean you can't use it, if you don't put a winter cover on you can use your evaporative cooler as a whole house fan to bring in fresh air.

A lot of people like to use their cooler during the holidays when they are entertaining; the house gets warm and stuffy. Just by turning the cooler on vent, you're able to bring outside temperatures inside and keep everybody comfortable without turning on the air conditioner.

How much moisture will an evaporative cooler add to my home?

Keep in mind that with an evaporative cooler the air in the home is changed every 2 to 3 minutes with fresh, clean, healthy air. Evaporative cooling is known as an open system, unlike central air conditioning that just recycles the same old stagnant air throughout the house, which is known as a closed system.

Evaporative coolers can add as much as 35% to 45 % moisture to your home. The ideal humidity range in your home should be between 35% and 60%.

Since Evaporative cooling is constantly circulating fresh air into your home you'll need some place for that air to go. We open up doors and windows to allow the air to circulate throughout the house and when we say "open doors and windows", we're talking only 4 to 6 inches in certain rooms where you want the cool air to go.

If proper air change is not obtained while running an evaporative cooler you can create an environment inside your home that's worse than outside, feeling sticky and humid.

Air conditioning is designed to extract all the moisture out of your home. Not only does it affect your home, but also your furniture, your skin and your body. That's why many of our clients complain of waking up in the morning with a sore throat or dry sinuses, and in some cases even waking up with a bloody nose due to the very dry climate it creates.

Evaporative cooling changes the air every 2 to 3 minutes with fresh, clean, healthy, and moist air, thereby enhancing the comfort of your home and your family. This actually gives you a cleaner and healthier home environment than central air conditioning can offer.

Evaporative cooling is an open system so you want to open doors and windows anywhere from 4 to 6 inches for optimal cooling.

After you get your windows set, there's a simple test you can do; we call the slam test. Go to the front door, open it up about 6 inches and let go.

If the door slams shut, you don't have enough doors or windows open. You want the door to slowly creep shut. When that happens, you have found the ideal indoor comfort for your evaporative cooling.

When the cooler is on high you will need to open your window spaces and door spaces a little further to allow for the increased volume of air to flow.

Failing to do this will increase the moisture in your home environment and cause a sticky feeling.

Do I need to replace my pads every year?

It's dependent on what type of system you have. For your basic swamp cooler, the type that takes Aspen pad filter media, it will need to be replaced every spring.

Aspen pads need to be replaced every year to ensure proper cooling in your home. Standard or high performance evaporative cooling systems utilize Celdek pads, and with proper maintenance you can clean these filters so they'll last anywhere from 4 to 6 years.

In high performance systems and standard systems you also should have an auto flush system installed. The auto flush system will control the alkali buildup in the water and help eliminate scales from building up and depositing on your filter media.

Maintenance and an auto flush system will keep your system running more efficient during the summer months, along with prolonging the life of the filter media.

Aspen pad filters need to be changed every year for best performance. Single inlet Celdek filters must be cleaned every year and with proper maintenance will last anywhere from 4 to 6 years.

In my home I keep my air conditioning thermostat set at 78-80 degrees. Will my evaporative cooler keep my house at that same temperature?

Most of the time your evaporative cooler can outperform the comfort of your central air conditioning at a fraction of the cost depending on outside temperatures. In our home, our thermostat stays around 76 degrees by either using our central air or our evaporative cooler.

We prefer to use the evaporative cooling for the simple fact that it adds fresh, clean, healthy air and it gives a cool energizing feeling that air conditioning does not.

Now, I'm a hot guy; I can't take even 78 degrees when using air conditioning. It makes me very uncomfortable. But, I can take 78 to 80 degrees in evaporative cooling all day long because of the moisture it provides; a cool refreshing waterfall feeling.

In fact, in my home during the summer, we sleep under blankets. At night my house will get down between 72 to 74 degrees with the evaporative cooling system running.

We tell our house guests, "Here's an extra blanket; it's going to snow in the house tonight." They laugh and in the morning they are delighted to have enjoyed a snuggly, warm, comfy bed during the summer.

Is a big cooler better to cool my house?

When people call and say, "I need to have an evaporative cooler and I want to get the biggest one possible." Bigger is not always better in this case. We use the four factor rule in determining what type of system would work best for you.

Two factors you have a choice of and two factors you don't have a choice of. The most important factor is; the home will determine what size of evaporative cooler it needs, though, normally the homeowner doesn't like that choice.

If a company comes in and wants to replace your last unit for the exact same size, they may be doing you a disservice because it could have been originally sized incorrectly. It's the home, the square footage, the ceiling, and where the cooler faces that will determine what type of system should be installed.

The second factor is city codes. You don't have a choice with this one. There are certain things that a licensed contractor has to do to stay within the county and city codes.

The third factor is the type of people you chose to do business with. Who's going to come in and install your system? Who's going to come in and service that system?

The fourth factor is what type of system I am going to have and what's it going to cost me. You pick the system that is best for you and your family.

The house determines the first two factors; you don't really have a choice about them. The last two factors are choices you as a homeowner get to make.

In evaporative cooling, bigger is not always better. You don't want to put in such a big evaporative cooler in your home that when it's turned on it blows small children or your beloved small dog out the door.

And you don't want it to be so big that you have to turn up the TV volume so loud the neighbors next door know what you're watching. We design systems so that 75 percent of the time you're able to run it on low speed.

Should I install an Evaporative Cooler in my Garage?

I get this question a lot. "Buff, we are part time residents here in the desert area and we like to leave our car here during the summer months while we go back to Canada.

What can I do to protect the leather, plastics, batters and rubber in my car? What kind of system can you install and is an evaporative cooler a good system to use?"

We do a lot of garages for that very reason. People leave a second car or have a golf cart in the garage when they go away for the summer. Or, even better yet, they may have a second refrigerator in the garage where they keep water, beer and soda pop. With an evaporative cooler in the garage we can keep that garage between 78 and 90 degrees on the worst day.

Keeping the garage cooled by an evaporative cooler will keep the leather, rubber, tires, and the batteries in your car or golf cart from deteriorating. It will keep the refrigerator running more efficiently so it doesn't cost so much. With garage coolers we recommend a timer over a thermostat to allow the system to have a drying out period over the evening.

It's a great idea to keep your garage comfortable, especially if you have a washer and dryer out there. So when mama goes out and does the washing, she doesn't melt. Don't you hate getting into a nice car with leather seats and while wearing shorts, then screaming bloody murder because you just burnt your fanny? Having an evaporative cooler in the garage is a great idea.

What is the difference between a swamp cooler and an evaporative cooler?

For many years swamp coolers were very popular as an alternative means of cooling. The way they got that name was because as the humidity started to rise the house would get muggy or swampy inside.

The weather outside needed to be very, very dry for swamp coolers to work. We're talking 5-10 percent humidity tops. When the humidity climbed up above that it usually started to turn very damp and moist inside the home, hence the title 'swamp cooler.'

Today there are high efficiency systems. The filter media is 12 inches thick; these are known as evaporative cooling systems or 'evaporative coolers.' The thicker the filter media the colder and the dryer the air is going to be when it enters your home.

Swamp coolers use 1 inch straw pads while evaporative coolers use an 8 to 12 inch rigid filter media that is going to give you better comfort and a greater range of temperature.

What type of maintenance does my evaporative cooler need?

Your evaporative cooler works very, very hard during the hard summer months to keep you and your family comfortable and unlike your automobile that needs service every three to five months we recommend your evaporative cooler gets serviced at least twice a year. Once in the spring time to get it tuned up to factory fresh condition for optimum performance during the summer.

We feel the most important service is the winterizing of your evaporative cooler. People ask, "Why do I have to winterize my cooler?" The number one reason is that we don't want water sitting in the metal cabinet for three to four months out of the year causing corrosion and rust.

There is also a possibility of bacteria building up within the system from stagnant standing water in the pan.

The spring start up is when it's completely serviced to get it ready for summer use. During the winterizing service we close it down and put it to bed to prolong the systems life, so you don't get bacteria buildup.

Yearly maintenance can save you money, time and comfort for many years to come; a small price to pay for peace of mind.

Notes:

_____

_____

_____

_____

_____

_____

_____

_____

_____

_____

_____

Phoenix Manufacturing, Inc.

www.evapcool.com

the **Dedication** to **Quality** & **Service**

Phoenix Manufacturing Incorporated is dedicated to providing the most efficient and cleanest technology available for all of our products and services. PMI has developed a world class technical center that will continue to aggressively develop new products with the most advanced technology available. These efforts lead to PMI providing not only the most efficient products available but those products of the highest quality. PMI continues to provide the highest level of service and customer response in the industry and we continue to refine and improve ourpolicies to meet all of our customer's demands with each interaction.

Mike Markowich
President

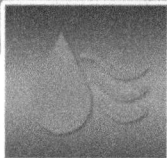

"It's Water. It's Air. It's two things you can't live without." **evapcool** ≈
by Phoenix Manufacturing, Inc.

About Phoenix Manufacturing

Value & Commitment

Phoenix Manufacturing is a designer, manufacturer, and distributor of evaporative cooling products designed for the comfort of the home or business. We build for both residential and industrial applications.

Values at Phoenix begin with our employees, customers, and suppliers. We strive each day to treat those involved with Phoenix with respect while performing our duties with integrity. We put a premium on those values to best serve our industry in a manner that will deliver quality in everything we do; phone calls, e-mail, meetings, along with the products and the service. They are designed to deliver our values as no one else does and to do it consistently each day.

Quality Products

For nearly 40 years we have manufactured in the United States, top quality evaporative coolers designed to meet every cooling need. From small personal cooling products to large 25,000 cfm industrial coolers, PMI sells the highest quality products with the longest warranties and backs the product they put into the market.

Company Values

At Phoenix Manufacturing we are dedicated to treating people with dignity and respect in all that we do by: Being honest, fair and consistent in all of our business dealings. Working to the highest level of business ethics in our business and encouraging each employee to pursue balance between work and personal time.

Our Brands -

Aerocool - Rigid Products -
http://www.evapcool.com/aerocool-rigid/

Commercial Product -
http://www.evapcool.com/aerocool-rigid/rigid-commercial/

Specialty Products -
http://www.evapcool.com/aerocool-rigid/rigid-specialty/

Residential Products -
http http://www.evapcool.com/aerocool-rigid/rigid-residential/

Frigiking – Aspen Products
http://www.evapcool.com/frigiking-aspen/

Commercial Product -
http://www.evapcool.com/frigiking-aspen/aspen-commercial/

Specialty Products -
http://www.evapcool.com/frigiking-aspen/aspen-specialty/

Residential Products -
http://www.evapcool.com/frigiking-aspen/aspen-residential/

What choices of evaporative cooling do we have?

Many different choices are available; window units, portable units, ducted roof mount units, all the way to large industrial units. There are also many types of media for each of the above cooler styles.

Save Green, Be Green with Evaporative Cooling

You have probably heard your friends and neighbors fondly talk

about their evaporative coolers, sometimes referred to as swamp coolers. You may have wondered what evaporative coolers are, and what makes them so special.

Evaporative cooling works on the principle of heat absorption by moisture evaporation. The evaporative cooler draws exterior air into special pads soaked with water, where the air is cooled by evaporation, then circulated into your space.

Evaporative cooling is most effective in climates relatively low in humidity such as the desert. The average annual humidity in Phoenix is 37%, making the Valley an ideal location to own an evaporative cooling system.

Also, anywhere along the southwest part of the country, Colorado, Texas or Southern California is ideal evaporative cooling locations.

Saving Green

Savings by using an evaporative cooler compared to a refrigerated air condition system is approximately 75%.

That can add up to quite a bit of money during the blazing summer months. The cost for installation is about half of that of central refrigerated air conditioning. The cost of maintenance is also lower with evaporated cooling because there are comparatively less mechanical parts, and no refrigerants to replace.

Being Green

Evaporative coolers use water instead of environmentally destructive and toxic chemicals found in refrigerants. Evaporative coolers conserve energy because there are no compressors so they only use about 25% of electricity that central refrigerated air conditioners use. The water vapor is recycled, so there is no waste.

Additional Benefits

Evaporative coolers provide fresh air circulating at all times, instead of recirculated, stagnant air as refrigerated air conditioners do. It increases humidity indoors, hydrating hair, skin, lungs, and sinuses.

The pads in evaporative cooling systems can provide a built in air filter, removing many contaminates found in the air pollution.

The good news is you don't have to choose. If you already have a central refrigerated air conditioner you can add an evaporative cooler to do the majority of the work during the year. You can supplement with your air conditioner during days of extreme heat and humidity, potentially saving thousands of dollars each year.

There are an entire line of residential Evapcool products, from window units to whole home units available for comparison on our website.

Evaporative cooling: How it works and why it saves you money

Evaporative cooling is actually a complicated phenomenon, dependent upon air and water temperature, air-flow and humidity or the amount of

water that already exists in the air. Although the physics behind this phenomenon are complex, it can be explained simply in laymen terms.

On an afternoon where it is 80°F and dry, a slight breeze can give you a chill; however on that same 80°F day, that same breeze will offer little relief if the conditions are humid. This has everything to do the ability of the air to accept the moisture that your body is producing through perspiration. On the dry day, the air can easily accept the water your body generates hence cooling you through evaporation.

Similarly, on the humid day, there is not enough room in the air to evaporate all of the additional water; hence it remains on the surface of your skin making you feel damp and clammy. Anything but cool!

Evaporative cooling can work almost anywhere, however it is most common and most efficient in dry climates for the reason stated above. Evaporative cooling was very popular in the Early American Southwest, when people would dip shear drapes in water and hang them in front of an open window.

The warm dry desert breeze would blow through the open windows, filter through the damp drapes and drop the air temperature to cool the space within the home. This same concept was employed in various inventions to move air through an evaporative cooling media and force the air into the living space.

However, the laws of physics still applied and hot humid conditions would prove a challenge. Eventually, the introduction of refrigerated air opened up booming industry that could provide adequate cooling regardless of the outdoor environment. Unfortunately, this technology came (and still comes) with a cost.

The cost of the refrigeration equipment is a multiple of the cost of an evaporative cooling counterpart. The cost of running a compressor and air handler can also be a multiple of the low cost of running an evaporative cooling system.

An Evaporative cooling system is relatively simple, although there are different types running at various efficiencies; the basic systems are similar in nature.

You need the following components in all systems:

Media: Some sort of material to saturate with water whereby the air can enter, pass through and be cooled via evaporation.

Means to Move Air: This is typically a fan or centrifugal blower powered by an electric motor. It moves the air through the media and forces it into the living space.

Means to Distribute Water to the Media: Systems vary slightly here where single pass systems simply use city water pressure to spread water across the top of the media; however the more popular systems have a reservoir, and use a small pump to recirculate the reservoir water over the media.

At Phoenix Manufacturing Inc., we are an evaporative cooler manufacturer and still cannot discount the comfort of a refrigerated system. However, there is no reason that both cannot be employed together. Most people that are Evaporative cooling advocates do exactly that.

In the early spring they run their Evaporative Cooler to provide comfort when their thermostat calls for cooling. In mid-summer, when the Monsoon season hits the deserts of Arizona, and the high humidity causes the evaporative cooler effectiveness to drop, they switch over to their refrigeration system.

The logic is that they have been kept comfortably cool during the dry season while saving **75%** of the electricity required to run their refrigeration systems. Hence they don't mind incurring a higher cost for a few weeks for the luxury of comfort. In a few weeks, once the high humidity has passed, they will switch back to Evaporation mode and continue to save money.

This is an extreme example in the deserts of the Southwest, however there are very dry climates where the temperatures do not get as high. Colorado, Utah and as far north as Fargo, North Dakota realize the benefits of evaporative cooling and even now use it as their only method for cooling during their summers.

This is just a simple example of how evaporative cooling works and how it is applied; but how does it save you money? The answer is simply evaporative cooling uses much less electricity to provide comfort than a refrigeration system.

For example:

A 1500sq.ft home with an 8ft high ceiling has 12,000 cubic feet of area to be cooled (1500 x 8 =12,000). A general rule of thumb, in the Desert Southwest is to change the air volume once every 2- minutes.

In other words, those 12,000 cubic feet of air must be completely purged from the home and replaced with cooled, fresh outside air. To do that, you need an air movement system with a capacity of 6,000 Cubic Feet per Minute (CFM).

A system such as that requires only a 1-HP motor and a small water pump. A 1-HP motor and the water pump combined consume 1.9Kw (Kilowatts).

That same 1500sq.ft home with an 8ft high ceiling requires 4-Tons of refrigerated cooling capacity. That system has a compressor motor and an air handler motor.

A typical 13-SEER, 4-Ton Refrigeration system compressor consumes 5.7Kw and the complementary Air handler consumes 1.8Kw. Combined they consume 7.5Kw.

1.9KW= 25% of 7.5Kw.

At a cost of $0.15 per Kwh (Kilowatts per Hour), the A/C systems costs $1.13 per hour to run where by the Evaporative cooler cost is only $0.26 per hour. Therein lies the savings!

Additional Benefits of Evaporative Cooling:

Evaporative Cooling (6000CFM)	Refrigeration (4-Ton)
• Approximately $3,500 Installed • Costs about $0.26 per hour to run • Brings in fresh outdoor air	• Approximate $8,000 Installed • Costs about $1.13 per hour to run • Recirculates stale indoor air

Efficiency Numbers: What they mean and how they relate to our various products

Evaporative Cooling Efficiency is the ratio of the actual cooling produced, to the energy required supplying it, relative to the  theoretical maximum that could be produced, expressed in percentage.

When discussing the efficiency of evaporative cooling media we are really focused on the actual temperature drop as the air passes through the media. In order to begin understanding this concept, you must first understand a few relevant terms:

Dry Bulb Temperature (Db): This is the ambient air temperature that surrounds you.

Wet Bulb Temperature (Dw): This is lowest temperature the air can attain by evaporating water into the air.

Wet Bulb Depression (ΔT): This is the difference between the Dry Bulb and Wet Bulb temperature. (Db – Dw=ΔT)

Efficiency (eff): This is a ratio of the actual air temperature drop across the media compared to the Wet Bulb Depression, expressed as a decimal percentage.

If the Wet Bulb Depression is 40 degrees and the actual temperature drop measured across the cooling media is

30 degrees, the cooling efficiency of the media is 75% (30/40 = .75).

This cooling efficiency is also known as the "Saturation Efficiency" because it refers to the amount of moisture that the media can evaporate into the air.

Water Usage: How it relates to our products

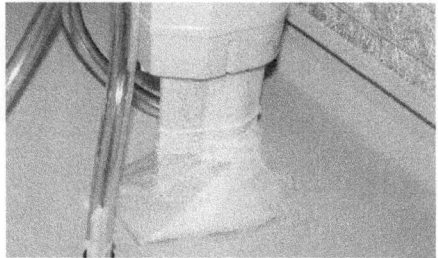

Water usage is as necessary to Evaporative Cooling as electricity is to refrigeration.

When discussing water usage, opponents of Evaporative Coolers, (Proponents of Refrigeration) often equate "Usage" to "Waste". This could never be farther from the truth! Water is a resource like many others in that it is 100% renewable after use in an evaporative cooler.

When the water is evaporated it leaves various solid compounds and elements such as calcium normally found in tap water in the cooler's reservoir.

That reservoir water is systematically purged and is perfectly fine to be used in watering your grass, garden, or trees.

After evaporation it is <u>not</u> irrevocably changed and returns to nature quickly and cleanly unlike other resources such as Petroleum or Natural Gas. That being said, let's discuss how water is used and managed in an evaporative cooler.

All evaporative coolers consume water via evaporation. This is what provides the cooling. The amount of water consumed by any given evaporative cooler can be expressed in a fairly simple equation.

In order to begin understanding this concept, you must first understand a few relevant terms:

1. **Dry Bulb Temperature (Db)**: This is the ambient air temperature that surrounds you.

2. **Wet Bulb Temperature (Dw)**: This is lowest temperature the air can attain by evaporating water into the air.

3. **Wet Bulb Depression (ΔT):** This is the difference between the Dry Bulb and Wet Bulb temperature. (Db – Dw=ΔT)

4. **Efficiency (eff)**: This is a ratio of the actual air temperature drop across the media compared to the Wet Bulb Depression, expressed as a decimal percentage. If the Wet Bulb Depression is 40 degrees and the actual temperature drop measured across the cooling media is 30 degrees, the cooling efficiency of the media is 75% (30/40 = .75). This cooling efficiency is also known as the "Saturation Efficiency" because it refers to the amount of moisture that the media can evaporate into the air.

5. **Cubic Feet per Minute (CFM)**: A number to express the volume and velocity of air movement.

6. **Gallons per Hour (GPH)**: A number to express volume and speed of water evaporated.

Now that we understand the terms, let's examine the equation for the rate of evaporation.

The rate that water evaporates is affected by the speed the air is passing through the media, the actual wet bulb depression and the efficiency of the media itself. For illustration purposes we will choose the following conditions:

- Db=100°F
- Wb=60°F
- ΔT=40°F
- Eff=93% (.93)
- CFM=6,000

This is the water that is actually evaporated but does not account for the "Purge Water" that is evacuated from the reservoir to maintain a clean media section. Please note that these values are in "Run Time Hours" not total hours in a day.

"Purge Water" is another necessary use for water in an evaporative cooler. As discussed earlier, when water is evaporated, it leaves behind the solid particles that do not evaporate. These particles include, but are not limited to Calcium and various salts.

These deposits, if left to collect in the system, can cause scaling and corrosion hence must be evacuated from the system periodically.

There are a few methods commonly used to satisfy this need and a few innovations only available from Phoenix Manufacturing.

These methods are as follows:

1. **<u>Bleed-Off</u>:** This method is one of the oldest and most common methods to reduce the buildup of minerals in the reservoirs. It is simply a capillary tube that allows a certain amount of water from the pump to be diverted from the media distribution assembly directly down the stand pipe drain. The rate of water typically relieved through this tube is 12oz/minute of cooler run time. Or approximately 720oz (4.7Gal)/hour of cooler run time. Although this is a widely accepted method, its flaw is that it is difficult for the average homeowner to regulate this rate based on the size of their cooler or the hardness of their water; hence it is the least economic from

a water usage standpoint and can use more water than actually required.

2. **Scheduled System Dump:** This is another very common method used by cooler manufacturers; however all "Scheduled Dump Systems" are NOT created equal and you will see a natural progression of innovations only available from Phoenix Manufacturing.

3.

    1. **Timer Method:** This method uses a timer to log the number of run time minutes and cycles a separate pump to run, after a predetermined run time, for a predetermined time period in an attempt to evacuate the reservoir. This method is used by many cooler & cooler parts manufacturers and is a more cost effective method than the "Bleed Off" method. It is more economical because it is not a constant bleed off and typically only evacuates the system once in an 8-hour period and then for only 7-minutes. At a flow rate of 4-Gal/minute, it only evacuates

28-Gal over an 8-hour period, OR 3.5-Gal/hour of cooler run time. This is a savings of 1.2-Gal as compared to the "Bleed-Off" method. This is an improvement, but still has some short comings. The problem with this method is in that although it is better than the "Bleed-Off" method, it still purges 28-Gal of water over a period of 8-hours of cooler run time.

2. **Programmable Drain System:** This innovation, only available from Phoenix Manufacturing, gives you the flexibility of selecting how often the system should purge and how long that purge should last. The frequency of how often the system should purge is based on the quality of the water supplied to the cooler. In areas with very hard water, the frequency of purging should be more frequent and less frequent where the water quality is better. Similarly, a small cooler may empty its reservoir in only 5-minutes where a larger

cooler requires closer to 9-minutes to empty. Only PMI gives you that flexibility with:

3. **Custom Clean™ (BDC100):** This accessory turns your simple recirculation pump into a state of the art Programmable Drain System. Simply plug your current recirculation or "Primary" pump into the specially designed Custom Clean ™ plug. Plug a secondary pump into the other end of the Custom Clean ™ and hook its hose to the included hose adapter and to the cooler drain. This system will record the hours of cooler run time and cycle the secondary drain pump based on the frequency and run time selected by you. With this system you can select a clean frequency of 2, 4, 6, or 8-hours as well as select a drain run time of 5 or 9-minutes. This flexibility ensures that you are using water more wisely and purging your system only as required. An added bonus of this design is that you do **NOT** need two

different types of pump! Two standard recirculating pumps perform both functions. This feature comes in handy in the event one pump fails and you are in a bind until you can get to the store to purchase a replacement. The primary pump is always the first to fail since it is used continually during the operation of the cooler while the secondary pump is only used during the purge cycle. Imagine a hot holiday party and your primary pump fails. Typically you would be without cooling until you replaced that pump. Since you have an identical pump as your secondary pump, you can simply switch pumps and get the cooler back on to keep the family gathering cool! The only drawback is you will not be able to drain the system until you replace that pump at least you remained cool until you could purchase a suitable replacement.

4. **Programmable Drain Pump (patent pending):** This innovation from Phoenix

Mfg., Inc. for release in 2014, takes all the features of the Custom Clean ™ and incorporates it into the body of the pump itself. It even has a "Continuous Run" mode in the event you need to swap it out with your primary pump as with the Custom Clean ™.

5. **<u>Programmable Drain Pump II (patent pending):</u>** This is the latest innovation from Phoenix Mfg., Inc. This is truly an intelligent water management system! Not only can this product be set to predetermined frequencies and run times with all the features of the Custom Clean ™, but it can actually measure the actual percentage of harmful minerals in the reservoir and purge based the system based on those values. No more guess work

Instructional Videos

http://www.evapcool.com/info-center/instructional-videos/

For more information

Phoenix Manufacturing, Inc.

http://www.evapcool.com

3655 East Roeser Road

Phoenix, AZ 85040

Phone:

602-437-1034

Fax:

602-437-4833

CHAPTER #12

122

Glossary

Note: Some of the terms in this book may have multiple meaning and uses. This glossary gives definitions only as they're used in this book.

Amps: An *amp* is a unit of electricity. Your evaporative cooler will use less amps then your air conditioning system which could decrease your utilities.

Aspen Pad Filters: Aspen wood is used in the

manufacturing of cooling media used for basic swamp coolers. Some say it looks like straw. This is the best filter media to use in basic swamp coolers.

Auto Flush System: A second pumping system installed within the evaporative cooler that has an internal timer to flush the water reservoir every 8 hours of operation time.

Automatic Back Draft Damper: Installed within the duct system of your evaporative cooling system to prevent air loss from your heating and air condition system. Opens and closes automatically.

Air Conditioner: A device that decreases the temperature and humidity of air which moves through it.

Air Cooler: Another term for an evaporative or swamp cooler. This type of device uses simple evaporation of water to cool the air.

Basic Swamp Cooler: Swamp coolers that use Aspen pad filter media. May have either three side panels or four side panels which hold the Aspen filter media.

Background Check: A process done at time of employment to ensure the safety of our customers. This includes checking criminal record, driving record, and drug testing.

BTU: "British Thermal Units" is a unit of energy used in the heating and cooling industry. In terms of air conditioners, this describes a unit's power and cooling capacity; the higher the BTU rating, the stronger the air conditioner.

Bearings: Two rotating supports placed between moving parts to allow them to move easily.

Belt: Also known as a V Drive belt; used to drive the main blower wheel in an evaporative cooler by connecting it to a motor.

CFM: An acronym for cubic feet per minute; can be used to measure the rate of air flow in an air conditioner or evaporative cooler.

Celdek Filter Media: A cardboard type ridged media used in single inlet units. This media could be 8", 12" or two 4" thick pads. These have a longer life span then Aspen filter media. They may last up to 5 years with proper maintenance.

Corrosion: A process of deterioration that takes place in metal when exposed to moisture for a long period of time.

Condensing Unit: Every split system cooling system contains two parts: the indoor coil/furnace/air handler and the outdoor condensing unit. The condensing unit typically contains the compressor and condenser coil (among other things).

Compressor: Often called the "workhorse" of an air conditioning cooling system. This refers to a pump that moves the refrigerant from the indoor evaporator to the condenser and back to the evaporator again; it circulates refrigerant.

Dual-Cool: A term that describes having both an evaporative cooler and a central air conditioning system in your home or business.

Ductwork: Channels or pipes that carry air throughout a home or building.

Down Draft: The direction the unit discharges the air through the duct system from the bottom of the unit.

Evaporation: The process by which water is converted from its liquid form to its vapor form; the basic working principle behind evaporative coolers.

Evaporative Cooler: Also known as a swamp or desert cooler; uses the simple process of evaporating water into the air to provide a natural and energy-efficient means of cooling; best suited for hot, dry areas with low humidity.

Filter: A device used to collect dust, dirt, and other particulates from the air; frequently employed by air conditioners and swamp coolers to improve air quality.

Filter Media: A term that describes the cooling media or pads used in evaporative cooling systems.

Float Valve: A mechanism that regulates fluid level by using a float to control the filling of water in the water tank; used in swamp coolers to regulate water levels.

Humidity: The amount of moisture in the air.

HVAC: An acronym for "Heating, Ventilation, and Air Conditioning." An HVAC system can also include moisture control and air cleaning.

High Performance Systems: Single Inlet Evaporative cooling systems that use either the 4 x 4 Celdek or 12" filter media for its cooling.

Operating Cost: The day-to-day cost of running your heating, cooling, or evaporative cooling equipment based on energy usage.

Pump: Main water pump that distributes water to the water distribution system wetting the filter media or pads.

Relative Humidity: The ratio of the amount of water vapor in the air at a specific temperature to the maximum amount that the air could hold at that temperature; normally expressed as a percentage.

Side Draft: The direction the unit discharges the air through the duct system from the side of the unit.

Slam Door Test: A way to measure the volume of air exiting the home or business when running the evaporative cooler. By opening the front door about 6" and releasing the door to see if it slams shut or creeps shut for proper air flow.

Swamp Cooler: Also known as an evaporative or air cooler; uses the simple process of evaporating water into the air to provide a natural and energy-efficient means of cooling; best suited for hot, dry areas with low humidity.

Synthetic Filter Media: Pad media made of green paper or blue synthetic material used instead of Aspen filter media. This does not have the cooling capacity of Aspen filter media.

Split System: A split system is one of the two types of system setups. A split system contains both an outdoor and an indoor component. Outdoor components include the outdoor air conditioner or heat pump condensing unit and the indoor components can include one, or a combination, of the following: evaporator coil, air handler or furnace.

Thermostat: A device used for regulating the temperature of a system so that the system's temperature is maintained near a desired set point temperature.

Timer: This is used to describe a device that turns on and off the unit; wonderful in controlling the sequence of the cooling process in garages and warehouses.

Up flow: High Performance evaporative cooling system that discharges the air from the top of the unit.

Variable Speed Motor: A type of fan motor used in some cooling systems that is designed to change its speed based on your cooling requirements. When used in conjunction with a thermostat, this helps keep the appropriate temperature air circulating throughout your home.

Water Control Valve: A mechanism that regulates fluid level by using a float to control the filling of water in the water tank; used in evaporative coolers and swamp coolers to regulate water levels.

Window Unit: Evaporative cooler that can be installed in a window or cut into the wall for a more secure installation.

Winterizing: Closing down the evaporative cooling system for winter. This service is important in extending the life of your evaporative cooler or swamp cooler.

Thank you for investing in
Your education by purchasing this book.

Register this book
& receive additional bonuses at:

www.EvaporativeCoolerBook.com